simpleSolutions

Kitchens

simpleSolutions
Kitchens

COLEEN CAHILL

Foreword by Gale C. Steves,
Editor-in-Chief, *Home Magazine*

FRIEDMAN/FAIRFAX
P U B L I S H E R S

Library of Congress Cataloging-in-Publication Data available
upon request.

ISBN 1-56799-927-1

EDITOR: Sharyn Rosart
ART DIRECTOR: Jeff Batzli
DESIGN: Lindgren/Fuller Design
PHOTO EDITOR: Wendy Missan & Lori Epstein
PRODUCTION MANAGER: Richela Fabian Morgan

Color separations by Colourscan Overseas Co. Pte-Ltd
Printed in Hong Kong by C&C Offset Printing Co., Ltd

10 9 8 7 6 5 4 3 2 1

Distributed by Sterling Publishing Company, Inc.
387 Park Avenue South
New York, NY 10016
Distributed in Canada by Sterling Publishing
Canadian Manda Group
One Atlantic Avenue, Suite 105
Toronto, Ontario, Canada M6K 3E7
Distributed in Australia by
Capricorn Link (Australia) Pty Ltd.
P. O. Box 6651
Baulkham Hills, Business Centre, NSW 2153, Australia

Acknowledgements

I'd like to thank several people for their enthusiasm, insight, and helpful advice: Tim Drew and Gale Steves at
Home Magazine, Christine Abbate, Timm Brandhorst, Brian and Chris Cahill, Maureen Cahill, and Leslie
Gross. And special thanks to Kate Perry and Sharyn Rosart at Friedman/Fairfax.

Contents

Foreword

Reduced to its defining function, the kitchen is a room with cooking facilities. And while this may have been a complete description at the turn of the last century, it barely scratches the surface of what the word evokes for us in the twenty-first century. Today, we want this space to meet a multitude of expectations. Of course, getting a meal on the table remains its core function, but now we're just as likely to see the kitchen as anything from a hospitable social center to an efficient home office. It's become the quintessential multipurpose room, rather like a high-tech version of the Colonial great room of our forebears.

Anyone who has ever confronted the challenge of creating a dream kitchen knows its nightmarish aspects: myriad details and multitudes of decisions. More than any other room in the house, getting the kitchen we want takes a lot of time, thought, and planning. With its built-in appliances, cabinetry, countertops, and tilework, a kitchen once finished doesn't offer the luxury of changing your mind after the fact. And to complicate the process even further, the room has to appeal to our sense of aesthetics. All in all, it's an impressive feat to come up with a successful finished project.

Long before getting bids from contractors or even before calling in a kitchen designer, start gathering ideas. The first step is to think about how you and your family really use the kitchen. Do several family members help with meal preparation? Should there be space for dining? Will it be an open space adjacent to a family room? Then, as you leaf through books and magazine articles, look at the details and decide whether they appeal to you and would fit your and your family's needs. Read the text; you'll find information about why and how the homeowners did things the way they did. Their experiences could present a solution you haven't thought of or an option you've never considered.

As you accumulate ideas, it's a good idea to organize them in files with headings such as "Appliances," "Countertops," "Sinks and Fixtures," and so on. At *Home Magazine*, we hope our readers will simply tear out the pages of the magazine for their files. Doing the same with a book seems a bit sacrilegious; fortunately, we live in an age of easily accessible photocopiers. In fact, the plus point is that you can put copies in different files if necessary. You might want to note the source and page number so you can easily find the original again.

In *Simple Solutions: Kitchens*, you will find a treasure trove of information and inspiration. More than just pretty pictures, it has the information and the tips you need to make wise decisions.

Congratulations. You are well on your way to making your dream kitchen a reality.

Gale C. Steves
Editor-in-Chief
Home Magazine

Introduction

The kitchen is one of the hardest-working rooms in a home. It has long been the center for meal preparation and food storage, but in the last few decades additional burdens have been placed on kitchens. They must accommodate growing families, take center stage during parties, impress the professional chef and, lately, join the technological revolution. That's a tall order for the humble kitchen. From the time when it was housed in a separate structure with food as its sole concern to the multi-functional room that is the literal and emotional center of the home today, it has been quite a journey for the kitchen.

In the last century alone, the kitchen has embraced a multitude of modern conveniences and has evolved with the changing role of women. The advent of electric appliances was followed by a host of gadgets designed expressly to save time. In the 1920s and '30s, kitchens began to expand to include cozy breakfast nooks, a sign of what was to come. Through the following decades, kitchens continued to grow larger and were reconfigured often to accommodate changing lifestyles.

By the end of the twentieth century, the kitchen walls literally came tumbling down. Cooking, dining, and relaxing were no longer separate activities taking place in separate rooms. Instead, the kitchen became the hub for everything from preparing meals to homework. Many would argue that the kitchen is the most popular and important room in the home today. If that is so, the kitchen has come full circle. There may no longer be the need to gather around an open flame for warmth, but the kitchen has returned to its roots as the heart of the home.

Perhaps more than any other room, a kitchen reflects the era in which it was built. It is easy to date a kitchen based on its equipment alone; indeed, the style of a refrigerator or range can be an almost exact dating measure. It is fun to look back on yesterday's styles—to see the subtle curves and rounded edges from an Art Deco kitchen give way to the right angles that followed. Yet a kitchen reveals much more than just its era. Like a life-size diorama, it represents the way people lived—how they cooked, where they ate, how they stored their food.

Today's kitchens are equally compelling and revealing about the way people live at the dawn of the twenty-first century. The quality that characterizes this generation is diversity. No two families are the same. Hence, no two kitchens are the same. In some families, there are two interested cooks and in others, none. Children quietly do homework at a kitchen desk in one home while across town an open plan combines the kitchen and family room into one lively space. Kitchens must keep pace with the times, and with the way people want to live.

This is no easy task. It helps explain why kitchens are often updated, refreshed, and remodeled. In new construction, the kitchen is always a critical room. To create the kitchen that's right for you, think about your lifestyle, not just about how you like to cook. First, you must think about the basic floor plan of your dream kitchen—for example, does an open kitchen suit your needs or do you perfer a kitchen that is a room unto itself? Next, think about larger questions of style, such as flooring materials and wall colors. There are also many smaller but essential details to consider. Do you need a built-in desk? A bookcase for cookbooks? A relaxed seating area? A place for the kids to play? As the functionality of the kitchen has expanded, so has the need for careful planning.

Despite the kitchen's role as a multi-purpose room, it still has one primary duty: it is a work center for preparing food. As such, the kitchen requires specific fixtures and materials. It's important to select appliances that suit your needs, and just as important to consider how they fit into the overall layout of the kitchen. In addition, sufficient storage space, adequate workstations, and efficient traffic flow are all essential to a comfortable, functional kitchen. Lighting is another element that can't be overlooked. Again, planning and preparation are the keys.

A kitchen that fails to meet your needs could be a recipe for disaster. That's why *Simple Solutions: Kitchens* was cooked up. You'll find solutions to everyday problems plus ideas that will inspire you to see your kitchen in a whole new light. The practical tips and helpful resources are a surefire way to create the kitchen of your choice—the one that reflects the way you live.

Open Kitchen Designs

As a hub for the entire family, the **open kitchen** is increasingly popular. Whether you like a combination kitchen/dining area or prefer a great room that includes kitchen, dining, and living spaces, there are things to consider before you start knocking down walls. When a room has to serve more than one purpose, there's bound to be more than one solution.

bright ideas

- Comfortable seating encourages socializing
- A single flooring material can unify space
- Island cabinets can be accessible from both sides
- Accent lighting highlights areas of interest

Open to a loft above, this rustic kitchen maximizes the natural light and uses color to create distinct work areas. With lots of counter space and plenty of room to move around, this kitchen can accommodate the entire family. ➲

This airy kitchen offers a great lesson in how architectural details can be used to define spaces. The design strikes a classical note with its crown moldings and Ionic columns that separate the kitchen from the living space. ↻

The multipurpose island serves as a divider and snack counter; it also conceals any clutter in the cooking area.

One way to make a kitchen seem larger is to widen or open up the entrance area leading into it. This kitchen is actually rather compact, but the wide opening between kitchen, dining, and living areas allows the spaces to merge, so the kitchen seems larger than it is. The overall effect is spacious and comfortable.

Bring unity to a multipurpose space with decorative details—here, a patterned chair rail draws the areas together.

In this home, careful placement of furniture has created distinct living, dining, and cooking areas, and yet all three remain open and traffic flows freely. ↻

Dividing a Kitchen

A wide-open space gains functionality when boundaries are introduced to differentiate **zones of activity**. For example, you may want to separate the work zone from the eating area. The division not only serves a **practical purpose**, it also creates an opportunity to incorporate an interesting architectural or decorative element.

A five-part transom frames this kitchen and creates an unobtrusive yet effective division between the cooking and dining areas—without blocking the flow of light into the room. ⟳

A large and lustrous wooden cupboard, placed within the arch, effectively creates two rooms out of one. The added storage and display space are an extra bonus for this kitchen. ↻

Accessible on both sides, the cupboard provides an attractive storage space for the living room, too. ➲

A marble-topped counter peninsula and white hanging cabinets separated by an arch offer a stylish yet practical way to divide a kitchen and adjacent eating area. The glass fronts on both sides of the cabinets allow light to pass through and provide access from either side. ↻

An architectural cutout can add interest and let in light.

A modern design helps define the cooking area in this kitchen while maintaining a sense of openness. The open shelving above creates a sleek display space. ➲

Smart design can work wonders in a small space. This modest yet very functional kitchen succeeds in clearly defining its cooking and dining areas. A sleek counter peninsula does the job and provides an efficient, uninterrupted work surface. ☊

Simple floor inlays can unobtrusively define a space.

Designed with a sweeping curve, the counter in this open kitchen creates a more dynamic division between the cooking and living areas. ↻

Relaxed Seating

One of the most welcome additions to the kitchen is **comfortable seating**. People like to gather in the kitchen before, during, and after meals—finally, they have a place to sit! For many families, the kitchen has replaced the living room. Great rooms afford the most bountiful solutions, but comfortable seating can be part of any size kitchen: look no farther than a cozy corner or sunny window.

This bi-level kitchen-dining area features a cozy breakfast nook—a perfect spot to eat a snack or to sit comfortably while visiting with the cook. ❶

Packing a lot into a small space, this galley kitchen opens to an area that includes both a dining table and a comfortable seating area. The upholstered cushions complement the intense blue of the kitchen cabinets, while yellow pine flooring ties all of the areas together. ➲

In this kitchen, a curvaceous sofa makes the most of the bay window. It offers an ideal spot to enjoy a relaxed breakfast or snack, to comfortably peruse a cookbook, or to socialize with the cook!

keep in mind

- ☐ Durable, printed fabrics stand up to daily use
- ☐ Wheels, casters, and swivel chairs add flexibility
- ☐ Built-in cozy window seats transform otherwise unused areas

Designed with two zones, this room includes an efficient cooking center that flows easily into a sitting area. A large island includes lots of storage and increases the available counter space. ↻

The small breakfast table slides in and out of the way when not in use.

Facing the cooking zone, the seating area features a fireplace and comfy furniture. The upholstered chairs are inviting and encourage people to visit with the cook while relaxing and without getting in the way. ☺

Universal Design

Universal design is characterized by accessibility; it leads to practical and creative solutions that benefit everyone, from children to the elderly. With so many people doing so many different things in the kitchen today, universal design has become important in every home. Improving the usability of your kitchen starts with an understanding of who uses it, and how it is used.

This kitchen is the result of a three-way merger: three small rooms—kitchen, breakfast nook, and laundry—joined forces to form one efficient kitchen. Family-friendly features like a microwave placed within easy reach, with storage below and a work area above, reveal the thought that went into planning the room. Frosted glass cupboard doors allow for identification of the contents without full disclosure.

Designed with the whole family in mind, this kitchen is a marvel of convenience and practicality, from the big picture to the details. Starting with the room's layout, the family chose a wide-open plan that makes all areas of the kitchen accessible while allowing easy passage through the space. ⋂

The microwave is positioned under the counter for easy access. Below it is a convenient storage drawer. ⊂

Instead of more counter space, this built-in table/work area was designed to be fully accessible, situated at a height that both young and old can easily manage. Glass-fronted cabinets and open shelves provide storage above the table. ➲

The island in this kitchen has been designed so that the work area is concentrated on one side only, away from traffic, with equipment within easy reach. Open shelving on the opposite side offers accessible storage. ↻

The dishwasher is raised off the floor for easier loading and unloading. It's also a good idea to keep the dishwasher within 36 inches (90cm) of the sink for easy reach.

keep in mind

☐ Vary counter heights for specific tasks

☐ Install appliances at convenient heights

☐ Plan open storage for easy accessibility

Although standard counter height is 36 inches (90cm), the baker in this family requested a lower-height, recessed area designed specifically for rolling out dough. ⋂

Traffic Flow

The **work triangle**—sometimes there are two—is the basic building block of a well-designed kitchen, and coordinating work and traffic is probably the biggest challenge of the well-designed kitchen. Whether a kitchen is spacious or cozy, the **flow of traffic** within and through it should be an important consideration upfront. There is such a thing as too much togetherness!

The work triangle in this kitchen is both efficient and spacious, with the refrigerator and sink both along the outside wall and the cooktop set into the island. All three are conveniently within reach. The curved island serves the important function of keeping traffic away from the work area; it has also been cleverly designed with a raised area for eating that is at once part of the kitchen but separated by the difference in height from the actual working counter space.

plan ahead

☐ Organize the room so that traffic patterns do not interfere with work areas

☐ Be sure to have at least 15 inches (37.5 cm) of countertop to one side of a built-in oven for placing dishes

This kitchen features two work triangles; fortunately, the floor space between work areas is wide enough to comfortably accommodate the flow of traffic. ↻

With an expanse of tile-topped workspace between the sink and the burners, this organization offers plenty of room for food prep. The bulk of storage, plus oven and refrigerator, sit on the opposite wall, effectively creating two practical work areas. ➲

Almost a perfect triangle, this efficient layout allows the cook to move around the kitchen in just a few steps. Since traffic doesn't need to pass through this kitchen, the full space can be devoted to food preparation. ∩

Especially in a big family or one with youngsters, it's a good idea to position the fridge where it can be accessed without disrupting the cook.

A classic work triangle, this arrangement of appliances, work surfaces, and storage allows for the most efficient use of time and space. Note that traffic is routed to the other side of the island. ➲

Space Planning

Planning ahead is the best way to ensure that your kitchen provides adequate space for specific tasks. There are general guidelines that can help determine how much space is required for different activities, like food prep. Once you've taken these into account, visualize how your family in particular uses the kitchen on a daily basis. (It's also worth considering how activity in the kitchen heats up during holidays or when entertaining.) Now you are ready to make the most out of the space you have.

bright ideas

- Develop your plan on paper (or computer) first
- Define areas for prep, cooking, eating, and clean-up
- Create at least one work triangle with the total distance between its three points less than 26 feet (7.8m)

Opting for a wall of windows meant that this kitchen would be flooded with light, but limited the number of wall-mounted cabinets. Since every square inch of wall space was precious, careful planning was necessary to meet the family's specific storage needs. ➲

A corner has been transformed into a beautifully organized storage center. The built-in wine rack is paired with open shelving that features dedicated spaces for dishes and a rack for wineglasses. ➲

Clever space-saving devices like the hanging spice and towel racks, condiment shelf, and cookbook rest are convenient, and prevent clutter on the counter. ☞

Optimum placement of the main kitchen sink allows for at least 18 inches (45cm) of counter space on one side and 24 inches (60cm) on the other.

The angled counter in this kitchen is extra deep, providing ample storage for china and serving pieces. The base cabinets feature beaded-glass doors that allow easy access to dishware from the breakfast area. ☞

This expansive kitchen has the room for a separate cooktop positioned to take advantage of the beautiful view, and plenty of space dedicated to a clean-up area. ☊

Cooktop placement guidelines recommend at least 9 inches (22.5cm) of counter space on one side and 15 inches (37.5cm) on the other.

A tiled alcove makes a lovely backdrop for the cooktop and forms the focal point of this kitchen. Four niches on the back wall and a shelf above stow seasonings that are frequently used. Maple butcher-block counters flank the cooktop. ☚

Sometimes open shelves or cubbies make more sense than a traditional cabinet. In this kitchen, in addition to the niches above the cooktop, an opening below it stows trays, cutting boards, and other over-sized items. Note more slots above the double oven. ☝

Small Space Kitchens

Fashioning an efficient kitchen from a small space requires careful planning—and creativity. Whether the kitchen is galley-style or an irregular shape, selecting the right spots for appliances and finding room for work and storage are essential. The best small kitchens go far beyond that, and can even outperform their bigger cousins.

bright ideas

▶ Monochromatic color scheme creates seamless space

▶ Creative storage contains clutter

▶ Natural light enhances openness

The choice of white paint for cabinets and appliances in this trim galley kitchen makes it appear larger. (Useful to know: white reflects 80% of available light.) The island along the right side provides added prep space and storage, while the windowed door at the end, which leads to a dining deck, lets in even more light. ➲

Placing the sink on an angle makes the most of this corner space and brings natural light into the kitchen, while offering a view as well. ↻

This cozy kitchen features open shelving above the sink, dividing the kitchen from the dining area, and providing easy access from either side. ⊙

This snug yet efficient kitchen packs a lot into a small space. The high ceilings allow custom cabinets to be fitted flush to the ceiling, increasing storage significantly. The shallow arc of the island provides a little more space around the cooktop. ⊃

A complete remodeling brought increased storage, new lighting and ventilation, and much more counter and display space to this small but efficient kitchen. ◖

By *choosing a side-by-side refrigerator/ freezer with a shallow depth (28 inches [70cm]), the family created enough space to include a washer/dryer.*

A single color for cabinetry at once unifies and seems to enlarge the space (note how the freestanding refrigerator/freezer appears built in and blends in with the cabinetry). ◓

Islands and Peninsulas

They come in all shapes and sizes, and it can be difficult to know what will work best in your kitchen. A **peninsula**, which is an L-shaped extension of the counter, or an **island**, which is a freestanding structure, can provide extra work space, separate cooking and eating areas, or serve as a spot for casual dining. Both play an important role in big and small kitchens alike.

This classic island encourages guests to talk with the cook yet keeps them clearly out of the way. Its top level is perfect for snacking and the lower level is just right for food prep. ●

A generous octagonal island is the centerpiece of this kitchen. It augments counter space and holds an auxiliary sink. The best thing about it is the way it draws people together for breakfast or conversation. ◑

This granite-topped island has been carefully designed with different levels for specific activities: the lower level, at 30 inches (75cm), is the right height for rolling out dough, a 36-inch- (90cm) high area is for everyday food prep, and the top level, with a height of 42 inches (105cm) flows into a butcher-block cutting board. ☝

The green-glass bar top on this two-level island reflects the light from the windows and twin skylights. The cook-top is placed on the island's lower level and allows the cook to look out at guests while preparing meals. ➲

Leave at least 12 to 19 inches (30—47.5cm) of space under countertop eating areas to accommodate legs.

plan ahead

Visualize in detail how
your family:

☐ Prepares food

☐ Accomplishes the
cooking

☐ Eats different meals

☐ Cleans and puts
away kitchen items

Triangular shapes
give this kitchen a
distinctive style.
The island, though
minimal, has room
for storage and
sinks. A trapezoidal
table complements
the island. ◗

With its whitewashed
cabinets, this island is
an unobtrusive yet
practical addition to the
kitchen. Though of
smaller proportions
than many, it never-
theless provides a
convenient work
surface, and grounds the
sturdy rack above, which
holds a serious cook's
heavy, commercial
cookware. ◗

A pot rack is perfectly placed above the island, where it is easily accessible yet stores pots and pans above the fray.

Oversized windows in this kitchen didn't leave much room for base cabinets. The ample island picks up the slack and houses the main sink. ↻

Freestanding Furniture

Regular furniture can find new purpose in an unfitted kitchen. A worktable can be as useful as an island, while adding country charm; a hutch may coexist happily with fitted cabinetry. An added benefit is the flexibility that comes with being able to move things around: not all the best kitchen solutions are nailed down!

An oversized, old-fashioned cabinet provides much-needed storage and adds to the retro style of this kitchen. The substantial work island, designed to appear unfitted, completes the look. ⊙

The antique table in this small country kitchen does double duty as a work surface and a dining table. ➲

The beauty of this worktable is that it can be wheeled to wherever it is needed—even out of the kitchen. The butcher-block surface can be called into duty as needed and drawers below provide extra storage. ↻

The two-drawer chest next to the oven offers another example of the charm of recycled or reconfigured pieces, particularly in a kitchen with an old-fashioned look.

In this unfitted country kitchen, an old table has found new life with a butcher-block surface and an auxiliary sink. Drawers and a lower level provide ample storage. ➲

This large and beautiful table has been given an auxiliary sink and a new surface suitable for its dual role as a food prep and eating station. Its long legs permit stools to be drawn up, and allow for full appreciation of the beautiful detailing on the wooden floor below.

Serious Cooking

Today, many kitchen appliances are available in **professional**-style versions. If you're passionate about cooking or frequently entertain, then investing in a kitchen that can stand up to the demands of **serious cooking** will be worth it. If you're not ready to make that commitment, there are still plenty of good ideas that can be borrowed from the commercial kitchen.

Almost everything in this kitchen is industrial-quality. The center island work area consists of several parts (some on wheels for easy maneuvering) and combines sturdy stainless steel with a butcher-block surface for cutting. Oversized storage areas below stow trays, pots, and pans. The appliances include a professional range, and a commercial refrigerator with freezer compartments. ➲

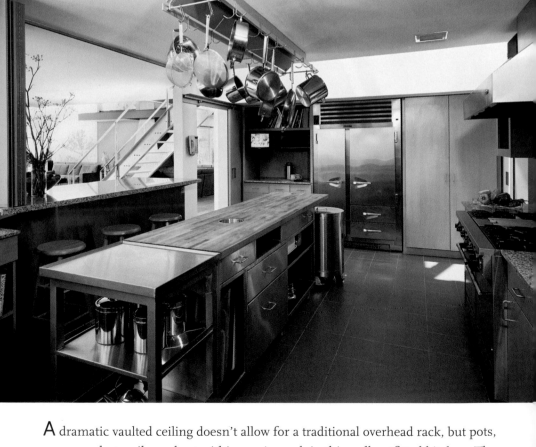

A dramatic vaulted ceiling doesn't allow for a traditional overhead rack, but pots, pans, and utensils are kept within arm's reach in this well-outfitted kitchen. The custom work island combines form and function, serving as an interesting divider and providing storage, display space, and plenty of work surface. ➲

Splashes of red brighten and soften the stainless steel used throughout this kitchen. The countertop is a continuous slab of stainless steel with an integral sink, making for easy cleanup. ➲

Industrial rubber flooring is super durable and easy on the feet.

When there are two cooks in a family, the kitchen has to work extra hard. Here, two stainless-steel ranges stand side by side, providing eight burners and two ovens. ↻

The area below this cooktop has been left open to allow room for oversized pots. ↻

This kitchen achieves a nice balance between performance and style. A pro-style double range in a bright hue is flanked by traditional maple cabinets, which provide both storage and counter surface. A wood-topped counter across from the range is a useful food prep area. ↻

plan ahead

☐ Double up on appliances

☐ Keep some storage open and accessible

☐ Install multiple sinks for quicker prep and cleanup

Kitchen Storage

Storage isn't just about finding a place to hide all your things. Adequate **storage** is essential for any kitchen, but well-designed storage will help create an **efficient** kitchen that's a pleasure to work in. Whether you're planning storage for appliances, food, or recyclables, don't forget to think about your future, as well as your current, storage needs.

bright ideas

- Appliance garages
- Pullout trash bin
- Tilt trays for sponges and scrubbers
- Roll-out shelves and bins
- Spice drawers
- Pullout appliance shelves

This clever pullout rack is ideal for oils and vinegars. Note its placement right next to the cooktop. ➲

Tile and wood are used to serene effect in this kitchen, which features a large center island containing closed cabinets and drawers, plus an open wine storage area that makes excellent use of the short side of the island. ∩

Fashioned from an antique cupboard, this work island contains plenty of storage. The opaque screened doors reveal shapes and silhouettes, but not the complete story. ➲

This country cabinet has a central open bay, a perfect spot to store colorful crockery that is used often. ◖

A massive built-in cupboard sets the decorative tone of the room, and provides both display and storage space. Baskets are at once decorative and useful, transforming open shelves into more drawerlike storage. ➲

Making the most of deep cabinets, shelves are mounted on the inside of the doors and doubled up on the interior to maximize nonperishable storage space. ⬆

Wicker baskets with wooden handles make excellent open vegetable bins. Planning early allowed the baskets to be integrated into the cabinets and fitted to slide in and out easily. ⬆

One trash bin is not enough in most households. Recyclables and pet food are separated and stored easily in this built-in unit that pulls out like a drawer. ➲

When space permits, a walk-in pantry is an excellent place to store foodstuffs. Open shelving of different heights accommodates most everything. ↻

Take note of the lighting on the inside of the pantry: it's a simple solution worth remembering.

This kitchen is filled with beautiful and functional details. In addition to the ample cupboards and large island, deep drawers keep cookware handy, and narrow space-saving pantry shelves are two-sided for double the storage. ➲

Pantry units pull out easily on heavy-duty slides. A strip across the shelf holds cans in place. ↻

Storage cabinets were designed to take full advantage of this kitchen's high ceilings. A "library" ladder makes these cupboards accessible, although they are best for items that are not needed everyday. ◖

A hutch becomes a cook's library with open shelves for books and magazines, plus a glass-fronted display space and closed cabinets and drawers for catchall storage. ➲

A niche beneath the built-in thermal convection oven houses a commercial cooling cart that can be rolled out when needed.

Above the auxiliary sink, glass-front cabinets and an open shelf for wine glasses create a "beverage bar" area.

Much of the wall space in this kitchen is devoted to storage. The combination of cabinets and drawers built in around the refrigerator allows for storage of everything from linens to small appliances. ➲

Displaying Your Wares

Not everything in a kitchen should be kept behind closed doors. Some items are easier to access when they are **displayed** out in the open, and showcasing collections is a great way to add a **personal touch** to your kitchen. Built-in cabinetry and shelves are ideal for customizing your kitchen so that you can display your wares within easy reach.

Cabinets have been eliminated to accommodate three traditional shelves supported by old-fashioned brackets, freeing up counter space and creating a stylish display area. ◖

Wall-mounted shelving above a built-in desk/work surface provides display space for a collection of Hall china and Fiesta ware. The moss-green accent color from the cabinetry is used on the wall unit and makes the colorful collection stand out. ➲

The transsom holds antique art pottery in a safe spot while adding interest to the doorway.

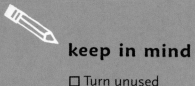

keep in mind

- ☐ Turn unused spaces above cabinets or doorways into display areas
- ☐ Use lighting in cabinets to highlight collections
- ☐ Rotate displays to keep the kitchen looking fresh

A kitchen step stool is a must whenever storage and displays are out of easy reach.

Display is integral to the design of this kitchen, and works at every level. A single shelf is set high above the windows, glass-fronted cabinets and open shelves are placed at eye level, and small cupboards and cubbies at counter height provide plenty of space to showcase things old and new—without clutter.

These cabinets were designed to suggest a cottage kitchen and there are plenty of nooks and crannies for display. Subtly bowed niches at ceiling height provide space for a collection of wooden houses (and wine storage). Above the doorway a deep shelf was added for the expanding collection. ➲

Flanking the cooktop are divided plate racks.

A wall-to-wall cabinet was designed specifically as a display unit to hold American art pottery in lighted, recessed arches. Tableware is displayed behind glass doors. ◖

Pull-out drawers below offer deeper storage for stowing packaged foods and other items.

Even a small area devoted to open shelving can make a big difference. Useful items are kept on the lower shelves while antique glassware is displayed above. ⊕

The top shelf reveals a small window—a cabinet would have hidden it and blocked the light.

White is the dominant theme in this kitchen. Staggered shelving in the center section allows taller items to be displayed and creates visual interest. This shelving is truly open, backed by white tile, not wood. ◑

Everyday clutter is stowed behind opaque sliding doors.

The open shelving in this galley kitchen looks as if it's floating in space. The effect is light and airy, while storage and display space is ample. ➲

Using Color

Color can create **mood** like nothing else. In the kitchen, color means more than just paint. Cabinets, tiles, and even appliances can get in on the color craze. Used boldly or with restraint, color can make a **strong statement**, help define spaces, or subtly influence the room's mood.

bright ideas

Try adding a splash of color to:

▶ One wall

▶ Moldings and trim

▶ Appliances

▶ Backsplash

The serenity of this spare kitchen is enhanced by the calm blue of the cabinetry. The wood stain works to offset the cool blue and add a dash of warmth. ➲

Bright colors are used sparingly yet definitively in this modern kitchen. Red mosaic tiles form the backsplash below monochromatic cabinets. A blue peninsula is bisected by a plane of wood. ➲

To create the unique brushstroke patterns that define this kitchen's look, the upper cabinets were stained with subtle stripes to complement the handmade tiles of the colorful backsplash tapestry. ↻

Texture and color come into play in this artistic kitchen where handcrafted quality combines with high tech materials to create a look that works beautifully. A palette of subtle hues warms up the cabinets and ceramic tiles. ↻

The front panel of the refrigerator was given the same paint treatment as the cabinetry, unifying the kitchen's design. ➲

keep in mind

- ☐ Yellows and reds stimulate the appetite
- ☐ Blues and greens have a soothing effect
- ☐ Neutrals are subtle and easy to live with
- ☐ White actually comes in many shades, from a soft gray-white to a bright yellow-white, to suit any mood

Barn red and warm brown tones were mixed to get just the right stain for the tongue-and-groove cabinets.

The palette of lively colors in this remodeled kitchen give it a warm and welcoming feeling. A pale "pea soup" green was chosen for the walls, and a light turquoise with darker trim was used on the ceiling to give the kitchen a more open feel.

The New Butler's Pantry

A traditional **butler's pantry** adapts readily to the needs of the modern family kitchen. Often nestled in a hall between dining room and kitchen, the pantry can offer **functional storage** and even serve as an **entertaining space**. An existing butler's pantry may need to be updated before it steps into its new role; otherwise, find an area within your kitchen to adapt or consider adding a pantry.

bright ideas

▶ Under-counter refrigerator

▶ Bar sink

▶ Built-in glass and plate racks

Situated right off the kitchen, this butler's pantry features a second sink, dishwasher, and under-counter refrigerator, which offer additional space to meet entertaining needs. The extra counter space serves as a coffee station. ➲

The pantry's style makes the most of its turn-of-the-century origins with new beadboard walls, crown moldings, and a leaded-glass window. ➲

A storage unit for glass and china is built into this butler's pantry. The deep counter can be used as a buffet or as a staging area to serve coffee, dessert, or after-dinner drinks. ↻

The stainless-steel bar sink is undermounted to the granite counter for easier clean-up.

The butler's pantry visible from this kitchen serves as an appliance station. A microwave is built in above, and ample storage is provided, making the area a very practical adjunct to the kitchen. ➲

Eating In

Eating is the very raison d'être of the kitchen, the main reward of all kitchen work. And today there are more and more variations on the **eat-in kitchen**. Breakfast, light meals, snacks, and even appetizers may be enjoyed at a counter, while a more traditional table is still (usually) the best venue for family meals. Whether you're planning a breakfast bar or want to create an **appealing dining area**, there are plenty of options.

bright ideas

▶ Install a banquette

▶ Large family? Try benches

▶ Upholstered chairs for comfort

▶ Child-sized dining table and chairs for kid-friendly eating

A long cherry counter is ideal for casual meals and invites guests into the heart of this kitchen. ⌒

Custom blinds allow diners to vary the intensity of the light, as well as providing privacy.

This breakfast area enjoys the benefits of the natural light that floods in through the enormous windows. The high-backed country bench and table give the effect of a built-in banquette, but the table and benches are actually freestanding pieces. 🎧

A sunny bay is a perfect spot to situate a breakfast table; the nearby counter serves as a convenient buffet area. ➲

An octagonal bay was added to this kitchen specifically to create a place for casual dining. The natural light and soaring ceiling make this location a delight for sharing a meal and visiting with guests. ➲

Mix and match comfortable chairs to add to the casual and comfortable nature of kitchen dining.

Two can comfortably enjoy casual meals at the counter in this kitchen. The hanging cabinet, originally part of a wall, provides storage without blocking any of the light, while under-cabinet bulbs light the butcher-block counter. ➲

The crescent-shaped bar top, attached to the island with pipe, is a perfect morning perch. The glass bar top seems to float and extends the island without taking up additional floor area. This is a clever way to add space for countertop eating to a kitchen. ◖

In a long, narrow kitchen it can be difficult to find the room for a dining table and multiple chairs. A banquette is a nice alternative. This one runs the width of the room and takes full advantage of the natural light, making it a pleasant place to sit any time of day. Comfortable, inviting, and versatile, this eating nook can also serve as a spot for homework, entertaining, or cookbook perusal. ☾

An L-shaped counter was designed to take advantage of the view. The lower height of the countertop and standard chairs makes it easy for children to seat themselves and enjoy a snack. ☊

The microwave turns this counter area into a snack zone. Kids can reach it on their own.

Overstuffed cushions create a sofa-like banquette in this comfortable corner. ◖

A built-in banquette is coupled with an old garden table refitted with a marble top to create a cozy breakfast niche that overlooks the yard. The wicker furniture, with its cheerful upholstered cushions, further enhances the gardenlike feeling. ◗

A large kitchen features seating at the counter for snacks and a banquette built into a delightful arched alcove. Cozy enough for breakfast yet large enough for a family dinner, the banquette is perfectly situated for easy access to everything in the kitchen. ◖

Communications Centers

T oday's kitchens are getting **wired**—not just for traditional high-tech cooking appliances, but for TVs, computers, and fax machines. Whether it's for homework, business, or just taking messages, adding an office or desk space to the kitchen makes a lot of sense. A great room may easily accommodate a full desk or large entertainment center, but with some clever planning, more modest kitchens can also find room for these new appliances.

bright ideas

- Under-cabinet electronics
- Drawers for hanging files
- Sliding tray for computer keyboard
- Wiring: electrical, cable, internet

A handy built-in desk occupies one wall of this kitchen without protruding into the room. Its surface is flush with the adjacent cupboards, and features the granite used throughout the kitchen. Below, file drawers can be locked. The cupboard next to . the desk holds a TV, VCR, and videos. ➲

There is no wasted space in this kitchen, which seamlessly combines old and new for maximum storage and workspace. Tucked away in the far corner is a compact office area with computer. ☊

Just beside the desk area is an under-counter washer and dryer: good space planning made it possible.

Radios (and other electronics) can be mounted under the counter to reduce clutter.

To make room for a work area, this kitchen annexed an unused corner and transformed it with built-ins. A small writing desk has two drawers below and open shelving above. The window makes this work area more pleasant. ☊

When there isn't room for a full desk, a compact area suffices. This built-in corner table is not exactly a desk, but it makes a useful work perch. Close to the phone, it serves as a mini workstation with space to write comfortably. ☊

This kitchen office area is around the corner from all the cooking activity and has a mini peninsula of its own that creates additional desk surface. ➲

Work Surfaces

Countertops are perhaps the **hardest-working** surfaces in the kitchen and they need to be both attractive and high-performing. Fortunately, the list of attractive and practical **materials** that can be used in today's kitchens keeps growing. There is no one perfect surface, but a review of your lifestyle, your budget, and the other materials featured in your kitchen is a good place to start.

A slate countertop complements the natural textures in this kitchen. As with most stones, color variations exist, so it's best to view a larger sample when making a selection. Slate can be porous and prone to staining so it's important to make sure it's been properly sealed. ◑

The first thing to know about concrete used for countertops is that it's not the same as sidewalk concrete. It is a lightweight composite to which color can be added. When it is cut and polished, it has the appearance and tactile quality of natural stone, as well as some of the same attributes, including durability and easy care. ⏻

Ceramic tile is supremely heat resistant and withstands water well. It's also available in an infinite array of colors and decorative styles. While the surface of tile is easy to wipe down, special attention must be paid to the grout between tiles, which can trap dirt and food residue. ○

Since ceramic tiles are not ideal for cutting, keep a cutting board handy.

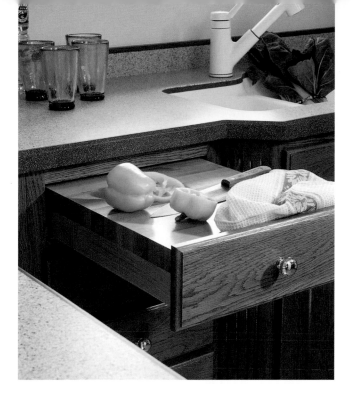

This chopping board-in-a-drawer is accessible when needed but otherwise out of the way: a smart and simple solution for food preparation. ⊂

One of the hottest surfaces today is cool stainless steel. Its seamless construction and easy cleanup make it a sanitary choice. Fit is very important with stainless steel. Since most stainless countertops will be custom fabricated, precise measurement and an experienced fabricator are essential. ☩

It's never a good idea to cut on stainless steel. It will scratch, and lesser grades can even rust: use a cutting board.

Marble and stone, both of which offer plenty of beautiful variations in color and texture, make top-notch kitchen surfaces. Granite, limestone, and slate are particularly good choices. A more affordable and flexible alternative to a single slab is cut tiles, though they will eventually require grouting. ☜

The dark, slab-like quality of this countertop offers a nice contrast to the light cabinets and serves as a bridge between the wood and the commercial range in stainless steel. ➲

One advantage of a stainless steel sink is that it is gentle on dropped dishware.

This built-in drain board is not only a useful feature to prevent pooling water, it also emphasizes the smooth texture of the countertop. ➲

Ventilation

Too often kitchen **ventilation** is one of the last issues to be considered. It really should be one of the first decisions. An adequate hood and ventilation **system** is essential in every kitchen to expel heat, smoke, and moisture, and to keep odors in check. There are a variety of venting options from **hoods** to down drafts and they're available in styles ranging from industrial to traditional.

plan ahead

▶ If a range is against an outside wall, a formula of 40 cfm (cubic feet per minute) per foot of range is recommended for exhaust fan capacity

▶ An island range requires a higher exhaust fan capacity (50 cfm per foot of range width)

Sunlight pours in through a window above the six-burner pro-style range. For illuminating the cooktop area, the range hood is equipped with interior lights. ➲

This kitchen features a medley of natural textures, including wood, stone, and copper. The gleaming range hood is not only practical but is an integral part of the room's design. ↻

The venting solution in this kitchen is incorporated into the room architecturally. The large chimney features wood molding and carved brackets that complement the cabinetry. ⭮

Old meets new in this kitchen, in which a vintage gas range has been restored to beef up burner output. It is paired with a new rounded stainless steel hood that complements the antique range while performing to today's standards. ⮑

Hoods have to be ducted to the outside.

Lighting

It is important to evaluate lighting needs before making decisions on fixtures. Even a kitchen flooded with natural light during the day will require additional ambient and task lighting. For a dramatic effect, use accent lighting. Proper lighting enhances a kitchen and makes it a pleasure to work in. Start with a review of how you work in your kitchen.

With a wall of windows to bring the outdoors in, this understated yet appealing kitchen is extremely bright and enjoys sunshine much of the year. Simple bare bulbs above the windows supplement the natural light and underscore the porchlike feeling. ⊙

Since the kitchen island is often the center of activity, it deserves special lighting. Here, three small pendants suspended above the island provide illumination. ◑

Other important work areas are lit directly from above with recessed bulbs.

Accent lighting above these cabinets highlights the subtle arch, while under-cabinet illumination gives an impression of depth and creates a dramatic look. ⊂

Recessed lights shine a direct beam to spotlight areas where intense illumination is needed.

For a soft glow, install rope or strip lights on top of cabinets, below them, or, if you have cabinets with glass doors, inside them. ⊂

Task lighting is usually desired at the counter, sink, and stove. In this kitchen, a combination of spots and under-cabinet lights provide the necessary illumination. Remember that the light should come from in front, rather than behind the task area, so shadows do not obscure it. ➲

The central ceiling fixture is a focal point of this kitchen and adds to its Arts and Crafts–style appeal. Providing bright ambient light, it offers general illumination that is supplemented by task lighting from ceiling spots. ◖

For a larger space, select a fixture that includes several bulbs, or "lamps," as they're known in the industry.

A pair of sconces that complement the ceiling fixture illuminate the sink area. ◑

A pair of pendant fixtures provide attractive lighting for the counter peninsula in this sleekly modern kitchen. Wherever close-up work is done—whether it's reading or chopping vegetables—task lighting is needed. ↻

This kitchen has plenty of natural general or indirect light from the windows and skylight, as well as several surface-mounted fixtures. Under-cabinet task lighting supplements the warm ambient light, illuminating shadowed areas. ⊃

Multi-Purpose Spaces

The kitchen often gives way to other workrooms like the laundry or mudroom. Integrating a variety of activities into one space can be a challenge. In addition to considering practical questions like plumbing, there are decorative issues, including finding clever ways to hide all that functionality.

The cabinetry from this kitchen extends into the dining alcove, where it fulfills multiple needs. An under-counter washer and dryer are easily accessible, while a tall utility cabinet stows cleaning supplies and appliances nearby. A second sink is tucked into the corner, while wall cabinets above provide storage for china and glassware. ↻

Decorative panels that match the cabinetry throughout the kitchen help the washer and dryer to blend in unobtrusively.

When this washer and dryer are needed, the decorative cupboard doors open and slide back out of the way. ↺

The granite countertop and tile backsplash not only extend the style of the kitchen, they are also practical solutions for a laundry area.

Resources

Professional Advice

There are many qualified professionals whose advice can be invaluable as you undertake a kitchen redesign.

American Institute of Architects (AIA)—If you are making structural changes, you would do well to consult an architect. Many architects belong to the American Institute of Architects. Call (202) 626-7300 for information and the phone number of your local chapter. www.aiaonline.com

The American Society of Interior Designers (ASID)—An interior designer can provide helpful advice, especially when you are remodeling an existing space. The American Society of Interior Designers represents over 20,000 professionally qualified interior designers. Call ASID's client referral service at (800) 775-ASID. www.asid.org

The National Kitchen and Bath Association (NKBA)—The National Kitchen and Bath Association certifies kitchen designers (CKD). They can provide full-service project management or design services. Call (800) 401-NKBA, extension 665, for a list of designers near you or write for more information: NKBA, 687 Willow Grove Street, Hackettstown, NJ 07840. The NKBA web site is also an excellent general resource for information: www.nkba.com

National Association of the Remodeling Industry (NARI)—When it's time to select a contractor to work on your kitchen project, you might consider a member of the National Association of the Remodeling Industry. Call (800) 611-6274 for more information. www.nari.org

National Association of Home Builders (NAHB)—If you are planning to construct a new home or build an addition, contact the National Association of Home Builders. Call (800) 368-5242 for more information. www.nahb.org;

Other Resources

The following manufacturers, associations, and resources may be helpful as you plan your kitchen:

APPLIANCES

Amana
(800) 843-0304
www.amana.com

Asko
(800) 367-2444
www.askousa.com

Caldera
(800) 725-7711
www.calderacorp.com

Dacor
(800) 793-0093
www.dacorappl.com

Dynasty Range
(800) 794-5233
www.dynastyrange.com

Fantech
(800) 747-1762
www.fantech-us.com

Five Star
(800) 553-7704
www.fivestarrange.com

Frigidaire
(800) 944-9044
www.frigidaire.com

Gaggenau
(800) 828-9165
www.gaggenau.com

Garland
(800) 424-2411
www.garland-group.com

General Electric
(800) 626-2000
www.ge.com

Jenn-Air
(800) 536- 6247
www.jennair.com

Kitchenaid
(800) 422-1230
www.kitchenaid.com

Miele
(800) 883-4537
www.miele.com

Sub-Zero
(800) 444-7820
www.subzero.com

Thermador
(800) 656-9226
www.thermador.com

Vent-A-Hood
(972) 235-5201
www.ventahood.com

Viking
(888) 845-4641
www.vikingrange.com

Whirlpool
(800) 253-1301
www.whirlpool.com

Wolf
(800) 366-9653
www.wolfrange.com

CABINETRY

Aristokraft
(812) 482-2527
www.aristokraft.com

KraftMaid
(800) 249-4321
www.kraftmaid.com

Merillat
(517) 263-0771
www.merillat.com

Wellborn
(800) 336-8040
www.wellborncabinet.com

Wood-Mode
www.wood-mode.com

FLOORING

Italian Trade Commission
Ceramic Tile Department
499 Park Avenue
New York NY 10022
(212) 980-1500
www.italtrade.com

Trade Commission of Spain
Ceramic Tile Department
2655 Le Jeune Road,
   Suite 114
Coral Gables, FL 33134
(305) 446-4387
www.tilespain.com

National Wood Flooring
   Association
16388 Westwoods
   Business Park
Ellisville, MO 63021
(800) 422-4556
www.woodfloors.org

www.floorfacts.com
(a global directory that helps consumers explore flooring options)

LIGHTING

American Lighting
 Association
P.O. Box 420288
Dallas, TX 75342-0288
(800) 274-4484
www.americanlightingassoc.
 com

PAINT

Benjamin Moore
(800) 6 PAINT 6
www.benjaminmoore.com

Pratt & Lambert
www.prattandlambert.com

Sherwin-Williams
(800) 474-3794
www.sherwin-williams.com

SINKS/FAUCETS

American Standard
(800) 524-9797
www.americanstandard-
 us.com

Delta
(800)345-DELTA
www.deltafaucet.com

Elkay
(630) 574-8484
www.elkay.com

Kohler
(800) 4 KOHLER
www.kohlerco.com

Moen
(800) BUY MOEN
www.moen.com

Price Pfister
(800) 732-8238
www.pricepfister.com

UNIVERSAL DESIGN

Center for Universal Design
North Carolina State
 University
Box 8613
Raleigh, NC 27695-8613
(800) 647-6777
www.design.ncsu.edu/cud

Universal Designers &
 Consultants
6 Grant Avenue
Takoma Park, MD 20912
(301) 270-2470
www.universaldesign.com

Adaptive Environments
374 Congress Street,
 Suite 301
Boston, MA 02210
(617) 695-1225
www.adaptenv.org

WINDOWS/DOORS

Andersen
(800) 426-4261
www.andersenwindows.com

Loewen
(800) 245-2295
www.loewen.com

Marvin
(800) 241-9450
www.marvin.com

Morgan
(800) 877-9482
www.morgandoors.com

Pella
(800) 54 PELLA
www.pella.com

Pozzi
(800) 257-9663
www.pozzi.com

Photo Credits

©**Laurie Black**: pp. 86–87 (Interior Design: Ellen Fitch Design), 87 top (Interior Design: Ellen Fitch Design), 87 bottom (Interior Design: Ellen Fitch Design); ©**Judith Bromley**: p. 18 (IKEA Design Service); ©**Steven Brooke**: pp. 22–23 (Architect: Stephen P. Herlong AIA; Interior Design: Nancy Gales of Southeastern Galleries), 40 top, 40 bottom (Architect: Deck House Inc.), 52 left (Design: Joan DesCombs CKD of Architectural Artworks, Inc.), 64 right (Architect: Barry Berkus AIA; Interior Design: Barbara Dalton ASID), 70 left (Design: Joan DesCombs CKD of Architectural Artworks, Inc.), 77 (Interior Design: Wikoff &Mestayer Inc.); ©**Grey Crawford**: pp. 51 (Kitchen Design: Matt Wolf), 65 (Kitchen Design: Karen Harautuneian of Hub of the House); ©**Mark Darley**: pp. 7 (Architect: Robin Pennell of Jarvis Architects), 74 (Architect: Robin Pennell of Jarvis Architects), 103 (Architect: Robin Pennell of Jarvis Architects), 104 right (Architect: Charlie Barnett AIA), 115 (Architect: Robin Pennell of Jarvis Architects), 116 (Architect: Charlie Barnett AIA); **Elizabeth Whiting Associates**: ©**Rodney Hyett/EWA**: pp.9, 17, 19, 63, 84, 85, 109 bottom, 119; ©**Neil Lorimer/EWA**: p. 71; ©**Tim Street-Porter/EWA**: pp. 2, 82–83; ©**David Frazier**: pp. 46–47 (Architect: Duo Dickinson), 76 (Kitchen and Interior Design: Patricia E. Gaylor), 95 (Interior Design: Patricia Stadel Interior Design); ©**Tim Fuller**: p. 97 bottom (Kitchen Design: Robin Rubin CKD & Katrina Terrell CKD of Hiline Designs, Ltd.); ©**Tria Giovan**: pp. 46 left, 70 top, 78–79; ©**Sam Gray**: p. 54 top (Architect: David Hornstein of Light House Design); ©**Kari Haavisto**: pp. 24, 25, 30 (Kitchen Design: Mark Wessels CKD of Herman-Johns & Associates), 31 (Architect: William Shaffer AIA), 52–53 (Design: Harry Fischman of Southampton Engineering), 60–61 (Architect: Cynthia Curley of Blue Bell Kitchens; Kitchen Design: Peter Cardamore of Blue Bell Kitchens), 75 top (Architect: John James), 92 (Kitchen Design: Mark Wessels CKD of Herman-Johns Associates), 96 top (Architect: William Shaffer AIA), 97 top (Architect: Jim Thomas; Kitchen Design: Charles F. Adams CKD of St. Charles of New York), 114 (House Design: Jim Zirkel; Interior Design: Suzanne Felber of Memory Merchandising); ©**Nancy Hill**: pp. 11 (Kitchen Design: Kitchens by Deane); ©**Michael Jensen**: pp. 14 (Architect: Thomas Bosworth AIA; Interior Design: Nanna Skalley), 20 (Architect: Jeff McClure of Ross & McClure Architects; Interior Design: Barbaba Murphy of Murphy Interiors), 44 (Architect: Thomas Bosworth AIA; Interior Design: Nanna Skalley), 81 (Architect: Jeff McClure of Ross & McClure Architects; Interior Design: Barbara Murphy of Murphy Interiors); ©**Chris Little**: p. 21; ©**David Livingston** (davidduncanlivingston.com): pp. 12 (Design: Kendall Wilkinson), 15 top, 15 bottom, 16 (Design: Robert Nebolon), 28 top (Kitchen Design: Acorn Kitchen & Bath), 28 bottom (Kitchen Design: Acorn Kitchen & Bath), 29, 32–33 (Kitchen Design: Acorn Kitchen & Bath), 34 (Design: Elma Gardner), 35 (Design: Elma Gardner), 36 left (Design: Bauerware), 36–37, 45, 49, 50 (Design: Starmark), 57 (Design: Kendall Wilkinson), 58, 59, 60, 61, 64 left, 66 (Kitchen Design: Golden Gate Kitchens), 68 top (Design: Beth Pachacki), 68 bottom (Design: Wilkinson Hartman), 69, 70 bottom, 75 bottom, 93, 98–99 (Architect: Cary Bernstein), 100 bottom, 105 (Kitchen Design: Kitchens & More), 106 (Design: Ken Burghardt), 109 top (Design: Starmark), 110 top (Kitchen Design: Signature Kitchens), 110 bottom, 111, 113 (Design: Ken Burghardt), 118 top (Design: Eugene Nahemow), 118 bottom, 120–121 (Kitchen Design: Golden Gate Kitchens), 121 right (Kitchen Design: Golden Gate Kitchens), 124 (Design: Lamperti Associates), 125 (Kitchen Design: Golden Gate Kitchens); ©**Bruce Martin**: pp. 88–89; ©**Deborah Mazzolini**: p. 41 (Architect: Stephen Muse FAIA); ©**Jeff McNamara**: pp. 80 top (Architect: Duo Dickinson; Architectural

Index